Teeny-Tiny Folktales

Compiled by
Jean Warren

Illustrated by Marion Hopping Ekberg
Flannelboard Patterns by Cora Bunn

Warren Publishing House, Inc.
P.O. Box 2250, Everett, WA 98203

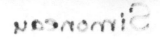

Editor: Elizabeth S. McKinnon
Production Editors: Brenda Mann Harrison
                            Gayle Bittinger
Cover Design: Larry Countryman

ISBN 0-911019-12-X

Library of Congress Catalog Card Number 86-051510
Printed in the United States of America

Contents

FOLKTALES

FLANNELBOARD PATTERNS

Introduction

Folktales have enchanted children since the beginning of time. Unfortunately, many of the tales are inappropriate for preschool-aged children because the stories are too long, too complicated or too frightening.

Consequently, we at Totline have endeavored to modernize the folktales in this collection to please our audience. It has been a real delight for us to select, to shorten and to adapt the tales for young listeners. On occasion, traditionally male-dominated tales have been rewritten to include female heroes and villains. It is our hope that such changes will ensure the continuation of these fine folktales in children's literature today.

Folktales are found in all cultures around the world. So for our collection, we have purposefully chosen tales from many different countries.

The flannelboard patterns that accompany the folktales are designed to be copied for home or school use. After being copied, the patterns can be cut out, colored and then backed with felt strips. The patterns can also be used to make cutouts from felt.

The finished flannelboard patterns can be used to illustrate or to tell the tales. (Additional shapes may be made to go along with the patterns, if desired.) One of the nice things about the flannelboard patterns is that they can also be used to develop language skills. As the children become familiar with the story characters, they can use the patterns to recreate the tales or to make up stories of their own.

Most of all, enjoy!

Jean Warren

Little Fox and the Tiger

A Chinese Folktale Adapted By
Elizabeth McKinnon

One day Little Fox was playing by herself in the forest when suddenly a tiger jumped out from behind a tree.

"Yum, yum," said the tiger. "I'm going to eat you up!"

Little Fox was frightened, but she kept her wits about her. In no time at all she had thought of a plan.

"I'm sorry, Mr. Tiger, but you can't eat me up," she said.

"And why not?" asked the tiger in surprise.

"Because I am very important," said Little Fox. "In fact, I am ruler of this forest. All the other animals are so afraid of me, they run away when I walk by."

The tiger was suspicious. "How can I be sure you are telling the truth?" he asked.

"That's easy," said Little Fox. "You follow behind me as I walk through the forest. Then you will see for yourself how important I am."

So Little Fox started off with the tiger walking behind her.

Soon they came across a deer playing among the trees. When the deer saw Little Fox, he paid no attention to her at all. But when he saw the tiger, he ran off into the bushes just like Little Fox thought he would.

"You see?" said Little Fox. "That deer is very afraid of me."

Next, Little Fox and the tiger came upon a wolf sitting outside his cave. Again, the wolf paid no attention to Little Fox. But when he saw the tiger walking behind her, he jumped up and ran inside his cave to hide.

"You see?" said Little Fox. "Even that big wolf is afraid of me."

The fox and the tiger continued on their way. Before long they came to a riverbank where a bear was fishing. Usually the bear was not afraid of anybody. He hardly even noticed Little Fox. But when he saw the tiger, he jumped into the river with a big splash and swam away as fast as he could.

"Now do you believe me?" asked Little Fox.

The tiger was completely fooled. He bowed down and said, "Forgive me, Little Fox. I had no idea you were so important. From now on I'll never bother you again."

So Little Fox went back to playing in the forest, feeling very pleased with herself for thinking of such a good trick.

The Funny Little Bunny Who Just Loved Honey

A European Folktale Adapted By
Jean Warren

Once upon a time there was a funny little bunny who spent every day looking for honey. Oh, he liked carrots and spinach, too. But Funny Little Bunny just loved honey!

Sometimes he was lucky and found honey in old trees. But most of the time he had to figure out ways to sneak into Mrs. Bear's cave where he could help himself to a pawful of honey from her big honey jar.

Now Mrs. Bear noticed that the honey in her big honey jar was going down and down. "Someone has been eating my honey, and I'm going to catch him," she said.

Mrs. Bear set a trap. She put the honey jar up on the top shelf and tipped it just a little so it would fall when it was touched.

The next day when Mrs. Bear went out hunting, Funny Little Bunny hopped into her cave. He saw the honey jar on the top shelf and climbed up to help himself. But when he reached inside to get some honey, the jar fell, Funny Little Bunny fell and the honey fell all over Funny Little Bunny!

Oh dear! Funny Little Bunny tried and tried to move, but the honey was so thick, he stuck to whatever he touched.

When Mrs. Bear came home, Funny Little Bunny was stuck to the floor. "Well now, see what I've caught," laughed Mrs. Bear. "It looks like I'll be having bunny stew for dinner tonight."

Mrs. Bear filled a large black pot with water and set it in the fireplace. Then she lit a fire under the pot and went outside to get some turnips and potatoes to put in her stew.

Funny Little Bunny tried and tried to run, but he was stuck fast. "Oh, if only I could get away, I would never steal honey again!" he cried.

As the fire under the black pot grew hotter and hotter, the honey all over Funny Little Bunny grew thinner and thinner. It started running down his long ears, over his head and down onto his little paws.

Soon Funny Little Bunny was able to move one foot, then another. Soon he was able to take one hop, then another. With a flip of his tail, Funny Little Bunny hopped right out of Mrs. Bear's cave and into the woods.

From that day on, Funny Little Bunny never ever ate honey. He just munched on carrots, spinach and lettuce like other bunnies do.

The Three Sillies

A Mexican Folktale Adapted By
Elizabeth McKinnon

Once upon a time Three Sillies sat down against a big tree to take a siesta. It was a hot day, so they pulled off their shoes and socks. Then they stretched out their legs, closed their eyes and went to sleep.

Now while they were napping, the Three Sillies got their legs all tangled together. When they awoke, they began to cry. "Boohoo! We can't get up! We don't know which feet belong to which! Boohoo! Boohoo!"

Just then a farmer happened to come along the road. "For goodness sakes!" he exclaimed. "Why are you sitting there crying like that?"

The Three Sillies cried even harder. "Boohoo! We can't get up! We don't know which feet belong to which!"

The farmer had never heard anything so silly in his whole life. "Stop your crying now," he said. "I'll show you which feet belong to which."

He took out a feather and began tickling the Sillies' feet. Tickle, tickle, tickle! Tickle, tickle, tickle!

"Tee-hee!" laughed the First Silly. "The feather is tickling my toes!"

"Those are your feet," said the farmer. "Pull them in."

"Tee-hee!" laughed the Second Silly. "The feather is tickling my heels!"

"Those are your feet," said the farmer. "Pull them in."

"Tee-hee!" laughed the Third Silly. "The feather is tickling my toes and my heels!"

"Those are your feet," said the farmer. "Pull them in."

One by one, the Three Sillies pulled in their feet. And one by one, up they jumped.

"Oh, thank you, Mr. Farmer!" they cried. "What would we have done without you? If you hadn't come along with your feather, we never would have known which feet belonged to which!"

Then the Three Sillies put on their shoes and socks, and off they went.

Lazy Jack

An English Folktale Adapted By
Elizabeth McKinnon

Once upon a time there was a boy who never did any work at all. People called him Lazy Jack.

One day his mother said, "It's not right for a boy to be so lazy. Tomorrow you must go out and find some work."

So the next day, which was Monday, Jack went to work for a neighbor. When the work was done, the neighbor gave Jack a penny. Jack started for home with the penny in his hand, but along the way he dropped it.

"Silly boy," said his mother. "You should have put it in your pocket."

"I'll do so next time," said Jack.

On Tuesday Jack went to work for a farmer who gave him a little pitcher of milk. Jack remembered what his mother had said. He put the pitcher in his pocket and started off on his way. But as he walked, the milk splashed out of the pitcher. By the time he got home, his clothes were soaking wet and the pitcher was empty.

"Silly boy," said his mother. "You should have carried it on your head."

"I'll do so next time," said Jack.

On Wednesday Jack went to work for a cheesemaker who gave him a soft cream cheese. Jack put the cheese on top of his head and started off on his way. But the sun was very hot. By the time he got home, the cheese had melted down all over his ears and face.

"Silly boy," said his mother. "You should have carried it in your hands."

"I'll do so next time," said Jack.

On Thursday Jack went to work for an old woman who had nothing to give him but a tomcat. Jack picked up the cat and carried it in his hands as he started off on his way. But the cat didn't like that. It scratched Jack's hands so much that he had to let it go.

"Silly boy," said Jack's mother when he got home. "You should have tied it with a string and led it along behind you."

"I'll do so next time," said Jack.

On Friday Jack went to work for a butcher who gave him a leg of lamb. Jack tied a string around the leg of lamb and pulled it behind him as he started off on his way. But the ground was all covered with dirt. And by the time Jack got home, the leg of lamb was all covered with dirt, too.

"Silly boy," said his mother. "You should have carried it on your shoulder."

"I'll do so next time," said Jack.

On Saturday Jack went to work for a farmer who gave him a donkey. It was hard work, but Jack finally got the donkey up on his shoulders and started off for home.

Along the way, he passed a house where a rich man lived with his daughter. The daughter was very beautiful, and she had a pretty smile. But she didn't know how to laugh.

Now the daughter happened to look out the window as Jack walked by with the donkey on his shoulders. It was such a funny sight that she burst out laughing for the very first time in her life. This made her father so happy that he asked Jack to be his daughter's husband.

So the two of them were married and went to live in a fine house. Lazy Jack became very rich and never had to do a day's work again. He invited his mother to come stay in his house, and they all lived happily together.

14

Little Bunny and the Crocodile

A Japanese Folktale Adapted By
Jean Warren

Once upon a time Little Bunny lived all by herself on a small island. Since she had no other rabbits to play with, she was very lonely.

Across the water was a big island that was filled with rabbits. Little Bunny spent her days watching the other rabbits and wishing that somehow she could get over to the big island.

One day Little Bunny saw a crocodile on the beach. His nice broad back gave Little Bunny an idea. "I will trick Mr. Crocodile into helping me get to the big island," she thought.

Little Bunny hopped up to the crocodile and said, "Mr. Crocodile, you swim all day in the water and I play all day on my island, so we don't know much about each other. I wonder which one of us has the most friends."

"Oh, I have the most friends," said the crocodile. "You can't see them now because they've all gone for a swim."

"If you lined up all your friends, would they reach as far as the big island?" asked Little Bunny.

"Yes, indeed," said the crocodile. "I will show you."

The crocodile swam off in search of the other crocodiles. When he returned, he lined up his crocodile friends between the big island and the small island.

"Oh, you do have many friends," said Little Bunny. "But just to make sure you have more friends than I do, I'd better count them."

Little Bunny hopped onto the back of the first crocodile. Then she began to count by hopping from the back of one crocodile to the back of the next. "One, two, three, four, five, six, seven, eight."

When Little Bunny reached the last crocodile, she hopped off onto the shore of the big island. Soon she was surrounded by many new rabbit friends.

When the crocodile swam over to the big island, he was very surprised. "You have a lot of friends, too, Little Bunny," he said. "I will count them. One, two, three, four, five, six, seven, eight, nine, ten!"

The crocodile smiled. "I was wrong, Little Bunny," he said. "You are the one who has the most friends. You are a very lucky little bunny."

"Yes, I am!" said Little Bunny. And off she hopped.

The Celebration

An American Indian Folktale Adapted By
Jean Warren

Tiny Flower pushed her head up through the ground. Was she too early for the celebration? No, for as she looked around, she saw many other flowers just arriving.

Throughout the winter Tiny Flower had dreamed of this day. It had been a long wait and a tiring struggle up through the cold, hard ground. But it had been worth it. Here she was, emerging into the Land of Light, surrounded by her new friends and anxious for the celebration to begin.

Mother Nature was also anxious. The flowers were arriving on time, but they still had their coats on. Everyone knew that the celebration could not begin until the flowers shed their coats and filled the world with color.

"Oh dear," sighed Mother Nature. "We can't have a celebration if everyone is all bundled up." She called for her children, the Wind, the Rain and the Sun. "Help me, children," she said. "Go out and greet the flowers and see if you can get them to take off their coats."

"I'll go first," said the Wind. He puffed up his cheeks and flew out to greet the flowers. He blew and blew as hard as he could, hoping to trick them by blowing off their coats. But the harder he blew, the tighter the flowers wrapped up. Finally he went back to his mother. "We'll have to call off the celebration," he said. "I can't get the flowers to take off their coats."

"Don't worry, Mother," said the Rain. "I know what to do." And, pitter-patter, pitter-patter, out he danced to greet the flowers. The Rain also had thought of a trick. He would fall so hard that the flowers' coats would become soaking wet. Then the flowers would have to take off their coats to dry. Down, down he poured, but the flowers only wrapped up tighter and tighter. At last the Rain, too, gave up. He went back to his mother and said, "It's no use. I did everything I could, but the flowers still have their coats on."

Then the Sun said, "Let me try. Perhaps I can *persuade* the flowers to take off their coats." And out he went to welcome them with his big, bright smile. Slowly the flowers began to warm up. They lifted their heads, stretched out their arms and smiled back at the Sun. As he continued to shine, the flowers grew warmer and warmer. Soon they got so hot that they tossed off their coats.

"Let the celebration begin!" announced Mother Nature as the world burst into color. All the animals rushed out to greet the flowers. The birds filled the air with songs, and the bees did dances of welcome.

Tiny Flower was enchanted with the Land of Light. It was even more wonderful than she had imagined. She felt like a queen with her many new friends, her crown of gold and her green velvet gown.

Before long the Wind and the Rain became Tiny Flower's friends, too. As time passed by, they learned that it was more fun being nice to the flowers than playing tricks on them. Tiny Flower loved dancing with the Wind, and she loved the Rain's soft showers. But most of all, she loved the Sun for his bright, warm smile.

The Little Old Lady and the Leprechaun

An Irish Folktale Adapted By
Elizabeth McKinnon

One day a little old lady was out walking when she heard a tiny little sound.

Tap, tap, tap. Tap, tap, tap.

"I wonder what that could be," said the little old lady.

She peeked behind a nearby tree. And there, to her surprise, she saw a leprechaun dressed all in green. He was tapping away with his little hammer, making shoes for the wee folk to wear.

The little old lady grabbed hold of the leprechaun's coat. "I've caught you now, Mr. Leprechaun!" she cried.

"Indeed you have," said the leprechaun calmly. "But I'll thank you to let me go so I can get on with my work."

"Oh, no," said the little old lady. "Not until you tell me where to find your gold. Everyone knows that when a leprechaun is caught, he has to show where his pot of gold is buried."

The leprechaun chuckled. "So, you want my pot of gold, do you? Very well. Just follow me and I'll show you."

The leprechaun started off with the little old lady holding tight to his coattails.

At last they came to a field where hundreds of bushes were growing. The leprechaun pointed to one of them and said, "Just dig under this bush and you'll find all the gold you want."

The little old lady looked at the hard ground. "I'll have to go home and get a shovel," she said. "But first I'll tie my red scarf on this bush. Then I'll know where to dig when I come back."

"That's a good idea," said the leprechaun with a twinkle in his eye. "Enjoy the gold when you find it!" And with a wave of his hand, he was gone.

The little old lady ran home and got a shovel. As she started back, she began thinking about how she would spend all her gold.

But when she reached the field, her eyes widened in surprise. Instead of one red scarf, she saw hundreds of them. Every single bush had a red scarf tied on it!

"Oh, no!" cried the little old lady. "That leprechaun tricked me! I can't dig under all these bushes. Now I'll have to go home without my pot of gold."

And so she did.

Mother Nature's Gift

An American Indian Folktale Adapted By
Jean Warren

One day while Mother Nature was out working in her garden, she heard the sound of angry voices. It was two of her children, the Sun and the Rain, arguing about which one of them was most important.

"I am the most important!" shouted the Sun. "Without me, nothing would grow!"

"No, I am the most important!" shouted the Rain. "Without me, nothing would grow!"

Back and forth they argued, each one sure that he was more important than the other.

At last Mother Nature grew tired of listening to them quarrel. To teach them a lesson, she sent the Sun to one side of the world and the Rain to the other side.

Soon there was peace and quiet again, and Mother Nature went back to her work. At first the Sun and the Rain didn't like being separated. But then they decided that this would be the perfect chance to prove which one of them was most important.

Day after day, the Sun shone down on one side of the world while the Rain poured down on the other. Before long the land on the Sun's side was dry and bare, and on the Rain's side there were terrible floods.

When the Sun and the Rain realized what they had done, they were sorry. They went back to Mother Nature and apologized. "We know now that neither of us is more important than the other," they said. "We need each other, and the world needs both of us to help the plants and animals grow."

Mother Nature was happy that the Sun and the Rain had learned their lesson. To celebrate, she decided to give the world a special gift.

Across the sky she painted an arc of beautiful colors — red, orange, yellow, green, blue and purple. "The world needs both my children, the Sun and the Rain," she said. "Whenever they decide to visit the world at the same time, this arc will appear in the sky. When the world sees the rainbow, it will know that my children are happy working together."

Why Mr. Bear Has a Short Tail

A Norwegian Folktale Adapted By
Jean Warren

One cold, frosty day Mr. Bear woke up early from his long winter's nap. He was very, very hungry. But the ground was still covered with snow, and Mr. Bear had a hard time finding food.

Now at that time, Mr. Bear had a long, bushy tail. Waving it behind him, he walked down to the river where he saw Mrs. Fox eating a big, juicy fish.

"Mmm, that looks good," said Mr. Bear. "Tell me, Mrs. Fox, how did you catch your fish? The river is all frozen over."

Mrs. Fox smiled slyly. "Oh, it was easy," she said. "First I made a small hole in the ice, then I stuck my tail down into the water. When I felt a pinch, I knew it was a fish biting, so I pulled out my tail and there was my fish."

"What a good idea," said Mr. Bear. "Could I do that, too?"

"Of course," said sly Mrs. Fox. "If you want more than one fish, just leave your tail in the water longer."

Mr. Bear was delighted with the thought of a fish dinner. He thanked Mrs. Fox and went out on the ice where he made a small hole. Then he stuck his long, bushy tail down through the hole into the water.

Soon Mr. Bear felt something pinch his tail. "Oh, I've caught a fish," he said. "But I'm so hungry, I could eat ten fish. I'd better wait a little while longer."

So Mr. Bear left his tail in the water. Before long he felt another pinch, then another and another. His tail hurt more and more, but Mr. Bear didn't mind. Soon he was going to have all the fish he could eat.

Finally Mr. Bear decided that he had caught enough fish. He started to pull out his tail, but his tail wouldn't budge. When he looked back over his shoulder, he saw that the hole in the ice had frozen over and that his tail was stuck fast.

"Oh, no!" cried Mr. Bear, "Mrs. Fox tricked me. The pinching I felt was not fish. It was the ice!"

Mr. Bear pulled and pulled until — snap! — off broke his long, bushy tail, leaving only a short stump.

And that is why to this day, Mr. Bear has such a short tail.

The Silly Wishes

A French Folktale Adapted By
Elizabeth McKinnon

Once upon a time a woodcutter lived with his wife in a little house at the edge of a forest.

The woodcutter had everything he needed, but he was always wishing for something more. And he was always grumbling because his wishes never came true. Grumble, grumble, grumble. That's all he did from morning to night.

One day when the woodcutter was working in the forest and grumbling, as usual, an elf popped out from behind a tree.

The woodcutter was very surprised. "Who are you and what do you want?" he asked.

"I am ruler of this forest, and I want some peace and quiet," said the elf. "I'm tired of listening to you grumble all day, so I am going to grant you your next three wishes. Just make sure that you choose them wisely."

The woodcutter was overjoyed. He ran home as fast as he could and told his wife the good news.

"How wonderful!" she cried. "You put some wood on the fire. Then we can sit down and make our three wishes."

So the woodcutter put some logs on the fire, and soon the orange flames were dancing and crackling in the fireplace. "My, what a fine fire," said the woodcutter. "I wish we had a nice sausage to roast over it."

Before the woodcutter realized what he had said, a big, fat sausage came bouncing across the room!

"Oh, you foolish man!" cried his wife. "Look what you have done. You could have wished for diamonds and rubies or even for a pot of gold. Instead, you wished for a sausage!"

"I'm sorry," said the woodcutter. "I didn't mean to do that. I'll make a better wish next time."

But his wife would not keep quiet. "A sausage! A sausage!" she scolded. "How could you ever have wished for a sausage?"

The woodcutter put his hands over his ears. "Enough about the sausage!" he cried. "I wish the silly thing would stick on the end of your nose!"

The words were barely out of his mouth when the sausage flew up and landed on his wife's nose where it stuck as tight as could be! The poor woman burst into tears.

"Oh dear! Oh dear!" said the woodcutter as he tried to comfort his wife. "I was going to wish that I was a king and then you would have been my queen. But whoever heard of a queen with a sausage growing on the end of her nose? Now I will have to use my last wish to make the sausage disappear." And so he did.

The woodcutter never became a king, but he learned an important lesson. From that day on, he began enjoying all the good things he had instead of wishing for more. He stopped his grumbling, and he and his wife lived happily ever after.

A Very Important Field Mouse

A Russian Folktale Adapted By
Jean Warren

Once upon a time there were two little field mice named Morris and Millie. Morris was a hard-working field mouse who hoped to marry Millie one day. Millie liked Morris, but she thought he was too small and too ordinary to be her husband. She wanted to marry someone big, strong and important.

"I know," said Millie,"I will marry the Sun." So she went to him and said, "Mr. Sun, you are the strongest and most important in all the world. Will you marry me?"

"Thank you for your offer," said the Sun. "But the Cloud is stronger and more important than I am. When he stands in front of me, I cannot reach the world at all."

"You're right," said Millie. "I never thought of that." So she went to the Cloud and said, "Mr. Cloud, you are the strongest and most important in all the world. Will you marry me?"

"I would be happy to marry you," said the Cloud. "But the Wind is stronger and more important than I am. All day long he pushes me across the sky and never lets me rest."

"You're right," said Millie. "I never thought of that." So she went to the Wind and said, "Mr. Wind, you are the strongest and most important in all the world. Will you marry me?"

"I would gladly take you for my wife," said the Wind. "But the Rock is stronger and more important than I am. No matter how hard I blow, I cannot move him."

You're right," said Millie. "I never thought of that." So she went to the Rock and said, "Mr. Rock, you are the strongest and most important in all the world. Will you marry me?"

"I'm sure you would make a very good wife," said the Rock. "But if you are looking for the strongest and most important, you need to find a small field mouse. Day after day he tunnels beneath me, never giving up his task. There is nothing I can do to stop him."

"You're right," said Millie. "I never thought of that. The field mouse is the strongest and most important of all!"

Millie went off in search of Morris and found him hard at work. She told him how sorry she was and how wrong she had been. "I know now that you don't have to be big to be strong and important," she said.

Soon Morris and Millie were married, and they lived happily ever after.

Little Rabbit and Tiny Bug With the Golden Wings

A Romanian Folktale Adapted By
Jean Warren

As the days grew warmer, Little Rabbit ventured out to greet the spring. "Every day I am growing," he thought. "I am getting bigger, stronger, quicker and braver. Why, I bet I'm the bravest animal in the whole forest!"

Just then Little Rabbit looked down and saw a tiny bug with golden wings. "Hello, Little Rabbit," she said. "Will you play with me?"

Little Rabbit thought, "I really am too important, too strong and too brave to play with such a tiny bug. But it might be fun. Perhaps I could play with her for just a few minutes."

So Little Rabbit and Tiny Bug With the Golden Wings began to play. First they played tag, then hide-and-go-seek and then follow-the-leader. Little Rabbit was having a wonderful time running, hopping and singing, while Tiny Bug With the Golden Wings was buzzing a merry tune.

Most of the forest animals enjoyed their music, except for Big Bear. Little Rabbit's singing had awakened him from his long winter's nap, and that made Big Bear mad.

"You woke me up, Little Rabbit," he growled. "Now I am very hungry, so I'm going to have you for my breakfast!" Then he reached out his long, furry arm and snatched up Little Rabbit by the back of the neck.

Little Rabbit didn't feel brave anymore as he peered helplessly into the angry face of Big Bear!

Tiny Bug With the Golden Wings knew that Little Rabbit was in trouble. "My friend needs me," she said. She flapped her tiny wings and headed straight for Big Bear.

Buzz, buzz, buzz! Buzz, buzz, buzz! Around and around Big Bear she flew until she landed smack in the middle of his nose!

Big Bear was furious. How dare such a tiny bug land on his nose? He swung out his paws to brush her away. But as he did so, Big Bear forgot about Little Rabbit and let him drop to the ground.

Little Rabbit landed on his feet and scampered away. But Tiny Bug With the Golden Wings kept buzzing around Big Bear until she saw that her friend was safe. Then off she flew to join him.

Together, Little Rabbit and Tiny Bug With the Golden Wings romped through the forest, each happy to have found a new friend.

Little Rabbit was right. Every day he was growing. And on that fine spring day, he grew a little wiser.

How Little Frog Tricked the Lion

An East Indian Folktale Adapted By
Elizabeth McKinnon

Once upon a time there was a lion who ruled over a large forest.

The lion was big and fierce, and all the other animals were afraid of him. Every morning they had to go out and find food for the lion to eat. Then they had to take the food to the lion's cave in time for his breakfast.

One morning Little Frog woke up very late. "Oh dear," she said. "I have no food for the lion to eat, and it's past his breakfast time. What shall I do?"

Little Frog thought and thought. She knew she had to go to the lion's cave. But if she didn't take him any food, he might swallow her up instead.

At last she had an idea. "I know," she said. "I will trick Mr. Lion into forgetting all about his breakfast." And, hop, hop, hop, hop, off she went to the lion's cave.

The lion was sitting outside his door, waiting. "You're late, Little Frog," he growled. "And where is my food?"

"Oh, Mr. Lion, the most terrible thing happened," said Little Frog. "When I was leaving my pond this morning, another lion jumped out at me and took the food I was bringing to you."

"What?" roared the lion. "Another lion in this forest?"

"Oh, yes," said Little Frog. "He had big yellow eyes, a long shaggy mane and sharp teeth just like yours."

The lion jumped to his feet. "Take me to your pond, Little Frog," he ordered. "I'll find that lion and chase him away!"

So, hop, hop, hop, hop, back to her pond went Little Frog with the lion following behind her.

When they got there, Little Frog pretended to look all around. "I don't see that lion anywhere," she said. "He must be hiding in the bottom of the pond."

The lion looked down into the water. And sure enough, he saw the face of a lion looking back at him. It had big yellow eyes, a long shaggy mane and sharp teeth just like his.

Of course, the lion was looking at the reflection of his own face in the water, but he didn't know that. He jumped at the face and SPLASH! He landed right in the middle of Little Frog's pond!

Oh, how foolish that lion felt. "There's no other lion in this pond!" he cried. "I've been tricked!" He was so embarrassed that he scrambled out of the water and ran away as fast as he could.

Little Frog was very pleased with herself. Her trick had worked! With a big smile, she hopped off to tell the other animals that the lion was gone and that now they could all play in peace.

Leopard's Drum

An African Folktale Adapted By
Elizabeth McKinnon

Long ago Leopard had a drum that was so big and grand, its sound could be heard all over the jungle.

BOOM, BOOM, BOOM! BOOM, BOOM, BOOM!

One day the Ruler of the Sky wanted to borrow Leopard's drum. He called all the other animals together and asked, "Who will go and get Leopard's drum for me?"

"I will!" said Elephant.

"I will!" said Tiger.

"I will!" said Zebra.

"I will!" said Crocodile.

One by one, the animals went off to Leopard's home. But when they saw Leopard's sharp teeth and claws, they were afraid. They ran back to the Ruler of the Sky. "Leopard is much too fierce for us," they said. "We couldn't get the drum."

Then Turtle stepped forward. "I will go and get the drum," she said.

All the other animals laughed. In those days Turtle had no shell. She was so weak and small, she couldn't possibly get the drum from a creature as fierce as Leopard.

But Turtle had a plan. When she got to Leopard's home, she called, "Oh, Mr. Leopard, have you heard the news? The Ruler of the Sky has a big, new drum. Everyone says it's much bigger and grander than yours!"

Leopard was so surprised to hear this, he forgot to be fierce.

"Nonsense!" he said. "No drum could be bigger or grander than mine!"

"They say that the Ruler of the Sky's drum is so big, he can hide inside it," said Turtle. "Your drum doesn't look that big."

"Oh, yes it is," said Leopard. "Just watch." And with that, he crawled inside the drum, pulling his long tail in behind him.

That was what Turtle had been waiting for. She stuck a big iron pot in the end of the drum so Leopard could not get out. Then she tied a rope around the drum and pulled it back to where the Ruler of the Sky and the other animals were waiting.

Inside the drum Leopard began pounding and kicking.

BOOM, BOOM, BOOM! BOOM, BOOM, BOOM!

"Let me out!" cried Leopard. "If you do, the Ruler of Sky can have my drum. And I promise to go away without hurting anyone."

So Turtle let Leopard out of the drum, and Leopard ran off into the jungle.

The Ruler of the Sky was so happy to have Leopard's drum that he offered to give Turtle anything she wanted.

Turtle looked at the other animals. They all had ways to protect themselves, but she had nothing. "What I'd like most of all is a hard shell," she said.

So the Ruler of the Sky put a shell on Turtle's back, and to this very day she is still wearing it.

Stone Soup

A Scandinavian Folktale Adapted By
Gayle Bittinger

Once upon a time there was an old woman who lived by herself in a little cottage.

One evening an old man came to her door. "Do you have food for a hungry old man to eat and a place for a tired old man to rest?" he asked.

"I suppose you could rest here for awhile," said the old woman. "But I have no food to eat."

"Well then, you must be very hungry," said the old man. "Lend me a pot, and I'll make stone soup for us both."

The old woman was very curious about the old man's stone soup, so she lent him a pot.

The old man filled the pot with water and set it over the fire. He took a large stone from his pocket, washed and dried it carefully and rubbed it three times. Then he placed the stone in the pot of water.

"If only I had a handful of flour, this soup would taste ever so much better," said the old man. "But there's no use thinking about what one hasn't got."

The old woman thought she might have a handful of flour. She went and found it and gave it to the old man, and he stirred it into the soup.

"If only I had a few small vegetables, this soup would be quite delicious," said the old man. "But there's no use thinking about what one hasn't got."

The old woman thought she might have a few small vegetables. She went and found them and gave them to the old man who stirred them into the soup.

"If only I had a bit of beef, this soup would be good enough for company," said the old man. "But there's no use thinking about what one hasn't got."

The old woman said she thought she might have a bit of beef, so she went and found it and added it to the soup. The old man kept stirring and stirring.

"If only I had a little barley and a drop of milk, this soup would be fit for a king," said the old man. "But there's no use thinking about what one hasn't got."

The old woman thought she might have a little barley and a drop of milk, so she went and found them. She gave them to the old man, and he slowly stirred them into the soup.

"Our soup is ready now," the old man announced. "We'll have a grand feast tonight."

The old woman was amazed. "Imagine," she said, "soup from a stone!"

Flannelboard Patterns

The following section contains flannelboard patterns to accompany each of the folktales in this book. The patterns are designed to be copied for noncommercial classroom or individual use.

Making Your Patterns:
- Trace the patterns or reproduce them on a copy machine.
- Color the copied patterns with crayons or felt-tip markers. (If desired, cover the colored patterns with clear, self-stick plastic for durability.) Then cut out the finished patterns and back them with felt strips.
- Or use copies of the patterns to make cutouts from felt. Glue on details cut from felt scraps or add details with felt-tip markers.

Using Your Patterns:
- Before reading a tale, arrange the finished patterns on your flannelboard to make an illustration for the children to enjoy looking at while they listen.
- Or place the patterns on your flannelboard as you read a tale to dramatize the action. As the children become familiar with the tale, let them move the patterns around on the flannelboard as you read.
- Later, let the children use the patterns to recreate the tales in their own words. Encourage them to use the story characters to make up original stories as well.

Little Fox and the Tiger

Little Fox and the Tiger

The Funny Little Bunny Who Just Loved Honey

The Funny Little Bunny Who Just Loved Honey

The Three Sillies

45

Lazy Jack

(For **Mother**, use pattern on p. 62.)

47

Lazy Jack

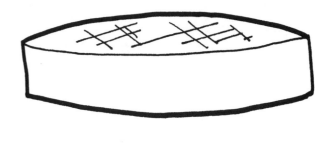

Little Bunny and the Crocodile

The Celebration

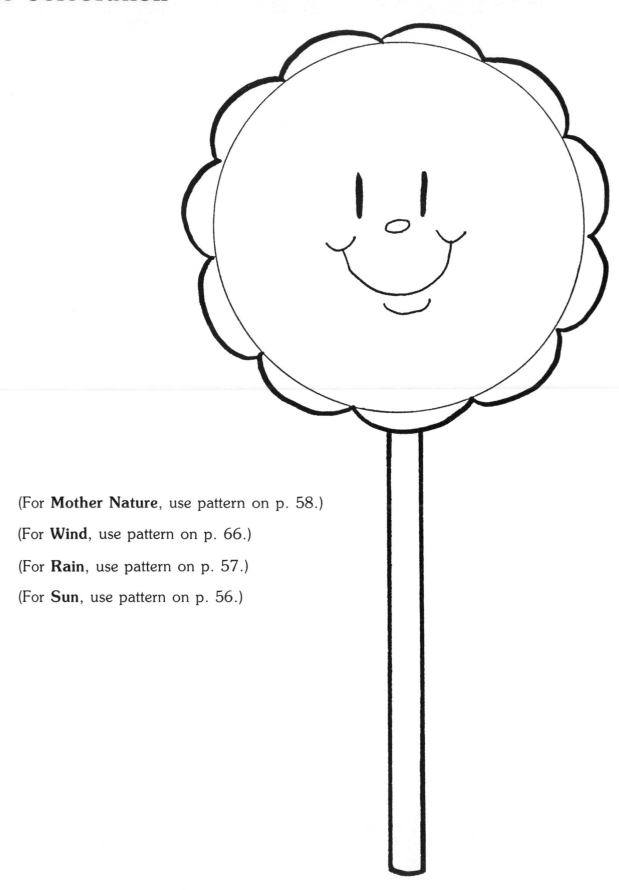

(For **Mother Nature**, use pattern on p. 58.)

(For **Wind**, use pattern on p. 66.)

(For **Rain**, use pattern on p. 57.)

(For **Sun**, use pattern on p. 56.)

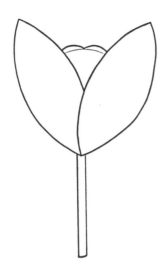

1. Cover flower face with leaves at the beginning of the story.

2. Move leaves down when the flowers toss off their coats.

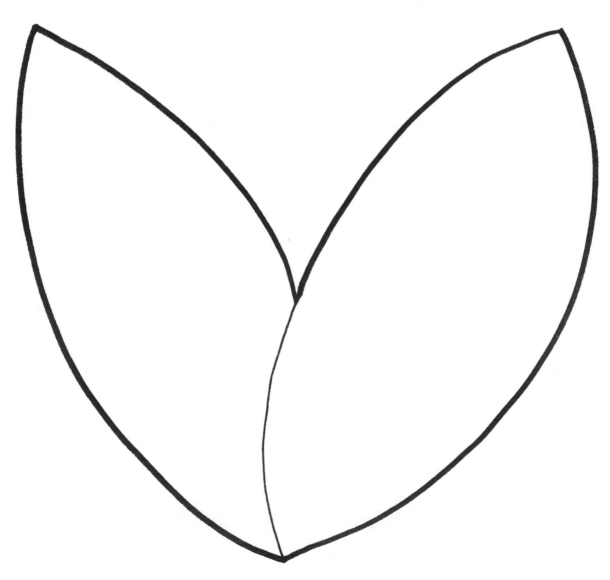

53

The Little Old Lady and the Leprechaun

The Little Old Lady and the Leprechaun

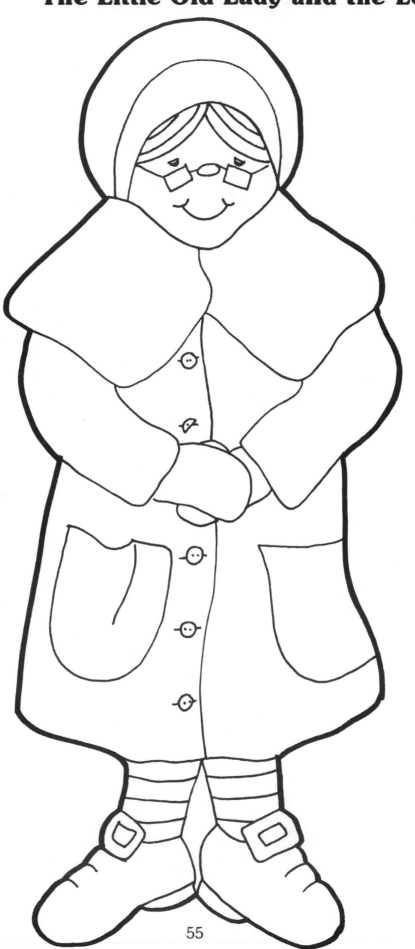

Mother Nature's Gift

Mother Nature's Gift

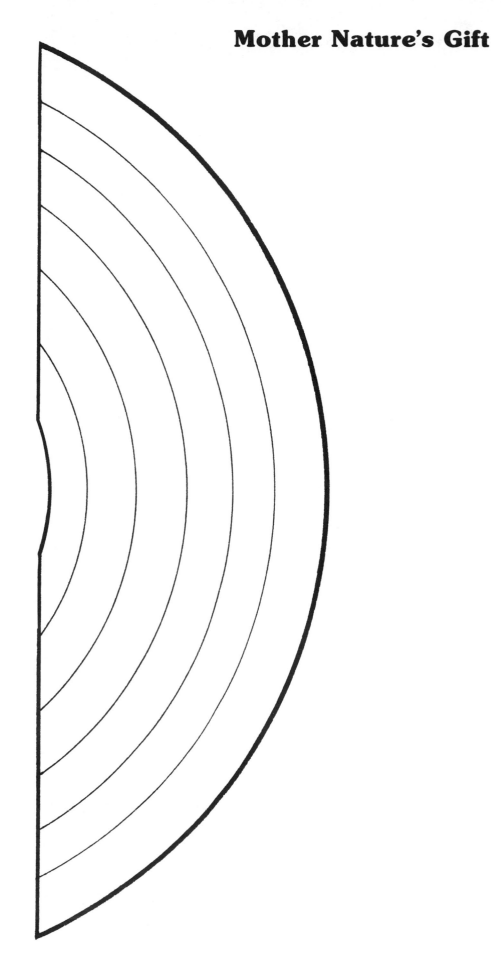

Why Mr. Bear Has a Short Tail

The Silly Wishes

(For **Elf**, use pattern on p. 54.)

A Very Important Field Mouse

66

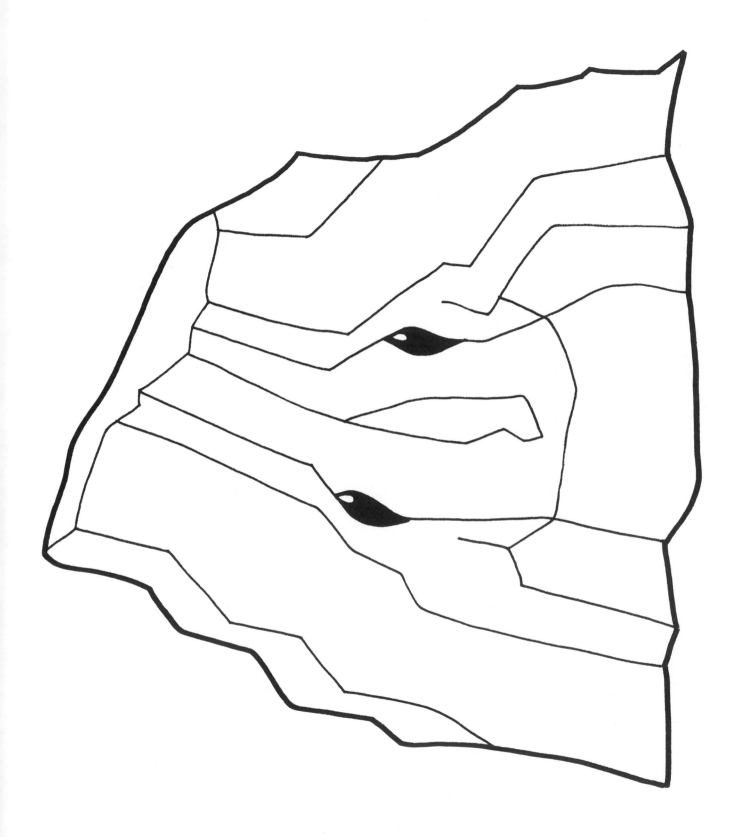

Little Rabbit and Tiny Bug
With the Golden Wings

69

How Little Frog Tricked the Lion

(Make a **pond** pattern by cutting out an oval shape about 11 inches long.
If desired, cut out an additional oval shape and glue a copy of the lion's face
on it to use for the pond in the last part of the story.)

Leopard's Drum

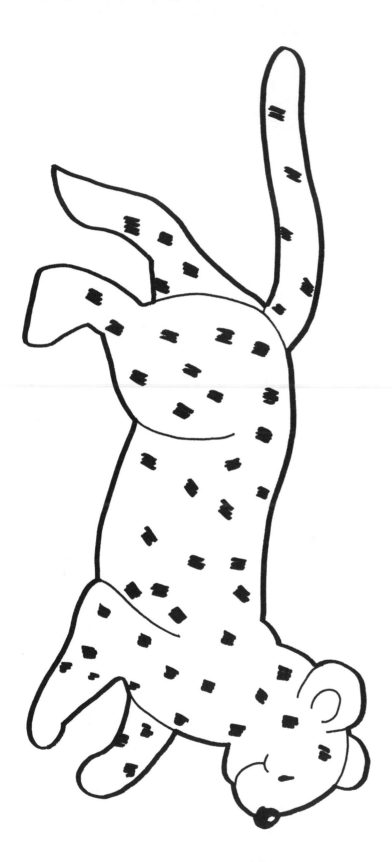

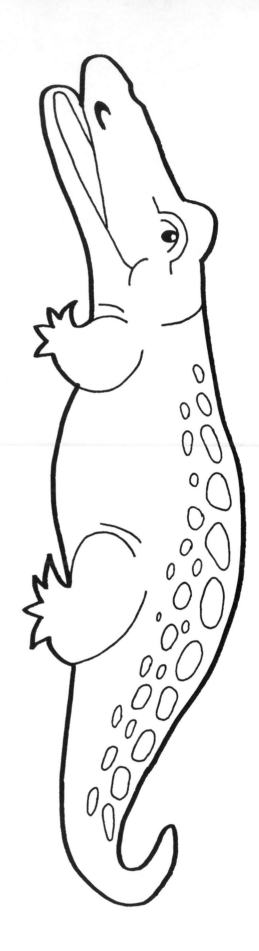

(For **Tiger**, use pattern on p. 38.)

Leopard's Drum

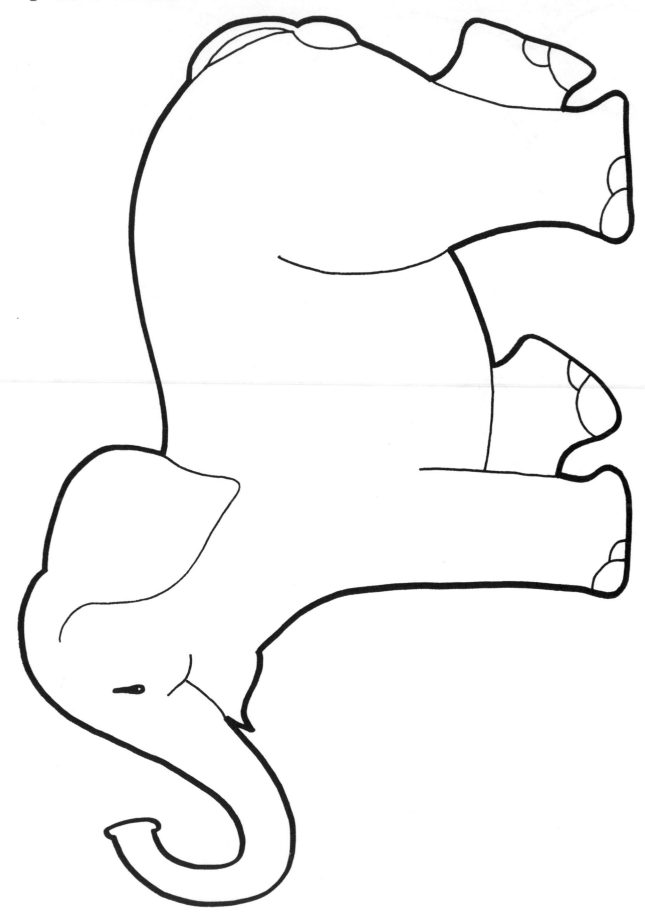

Stone Soup

Stone Soup

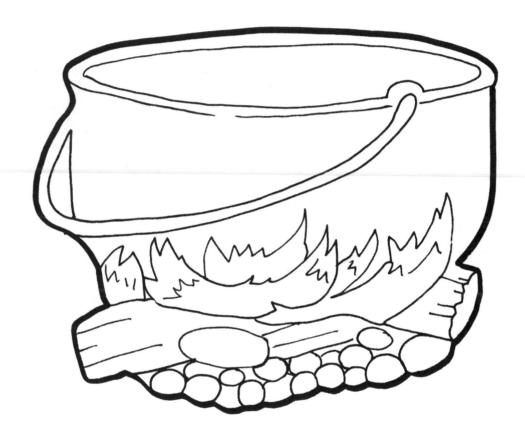

Totline® newsletter. Page for page, the

Totline has more usable activities than any other early

childhood education newsletter.

Each bimonthly issue offers chal-

lenging and creative hands-on

activities for children ages 2 to 6.

Each issue of this indispensable

resource includes suggestions for

♦ seasonal themes ♦ learning games ♦ music and

movement ♦ open-ended art ♦ language skills ♦ fun

science adventures ♦ reproducible patterns ♦ repro-

ducible parent-flyer pages. **SAMPLE ISSUE: $2.**

Super Snack News. This reproducible

monthly newsletter is designed for parents. Each 4-page

issue is filled with ♦ nutritious

snack recipes ♦ health tips ♦ and

seasonal activities, including art,

games, songs, and rhymes. Also

included are portion guidelines

for the CACFP government pro-

gram. With each subscription you are given the right to

make up to 200 copies. *Super Snack News* is great for

parent involvement! **SAMPLE ISSUE: $1.**

Hands-on, creative teaching ideas from Totline books

PIGGYBACK® SONG SERIES

Piggyback Songs
More Piggyback Songs
Piggyback Songs for Infants and Toddlers
Piggyback Songs in Praise of God
Piggyback Songs in Praise of Jesus
Holiday Piggyback Songs
Animal Piggyback Songs
Piggyback Songs for School
Piggyback Songs to Sign

1•2•3 SERIES

1•2•3 Art
1•2•3 Games
1•2•3 Colors
1•2•3 Puppets
1•2•3 Murals
1•2•3 Books
1•2•3 Reading & Writing
1•2•3 Rhymes, Stories & Songs
1•2•3 Math
1•2•3 Science

MIX & MATCH PATTERNS

Animal Patterns
Everyday Patterns
Holiday Patterns
Nature Patterns

CUT & TELL SERIES

Scissor Stories for Fall
Scissor Stories for Winter
Scissor Stories for Spring

TEACHING TALE SERIES

Teeny-Tiny Folktales
Short-Short Stories
Mini-Mini Musicals

TAKE-HOME SERIES

Alphabet & Number Rhymes
Color, Shape & Season Rhymes
Object Rhymes
Animal Rhymes

THEME-A-SAURUS® SERIES

Theme-A-Saurus
Theme-A-Saurus II
Toddler Theme-A-Saurus
Alphabet Theme-A-Saurus
Nursery Rhyme Theme-A-Saurus
Storytime Theme-A-Saurus

EXPLORING SERIES

Exploring Sand
Exploring Water
Exploring Wood

CELEBRATION SERIES

Small World Celebrations
Special Day Celebrations
Yankee Doodle Birthday Celebrations
Great Big Holiday Celebrations

LEARNING & CARING ABOUT

Our World
Our Selves
Our Town

1001 SERIES

1001 Teaching Props
1001 Teaching Tips
1001 Rhymes

ABC SERIES

ABC Space
ABC Farm
ABC Zoo
ABC Circus

PLAY & LEARN SERIES

Play & Learn with Magnets
Play & Learn with Rubber Stamps

OTHER

Super Snacks
Healthy Snacks
Teaching Snacks
Celebrating Childhood
Home Activity Booklet
23 Hands-On Workshops
Cooperation Booklet

Totline books are available at school-supply and parent-teacher stores.

Warren Publishing House, Inc.